LEADERSHIP

LEADERSHIP IN COUNTRY

TAMANA TAMANA

- ACKNOWLEDEGMENT

LEADERSHIP IS NOT POWER IT IS ABOUT RESPONSIBILITY. a good leader enligtens the country .

Leaders of the world and of any country particular plays most important role to achieve genuine happiness of its people. Good and capable leader leads its people and country to a peace and prosperity, while the cruel and incapable leader bring people to the world of sufferings and ultimately ruin country.

Leader must not only be educated and experienced but it is important to be a compassionate and sensible to the problems faced by their people. Leaders of the government should win the trust of people by being strategically friendly avoiding any kind of provocation or war with neighboring countries and must also allow a degree of transparency in the day to day working and the governance of the country.

Contents

CHAPTER ONE

- **Introduction to Leadership:**

It is a characteristic of every group whether small or big to have a leader. The phenomenon of leadership is evidenced in the play of children, in the games of adults, in trade unions in an industry and in several other situations. The moral is that groups need leaders if they are to pull together as a team.

How leadership evolves has been a controversial problem and students of human affairs in spite of their efforts to evaluate the role of leaders in group behavior, have not come to any final agreement.

ADVERTISEMENTS:

Leaders are either necessary or history is made by them or leaders are merely the expression of popular needs. The first view is called the "leader principle" or the "great-man theory" of history. It holds that people drift along in aimless confusion until a gifted leader assumes command and tells them what to do. He may accomplish social change for good or bad, but the truth is that he appears to accomplish much more than he actually does.

For example, Hitler is said to have killed millions of people, but literally speaking, he himself did not kill them and yet he is credited with such events as killing and conquering. The second view is the sociological view.

It says that history makes or selects the man, and not vice versa. Social and cultural developments are thought to follow their own laws, and the presence of a particular person as leader is purely coincidental.

For example, if a society is at war, a peaceful leader will not be tolerated; in other words, every leader has to follow the needs of the group. In brief, sometimes the leader acquires the leadership influence as a result of his assigned role in an already structured group according to the needs of the group. Sometimes, the group has no predetermined structure and the leader emerges from the group.

2. Definition of Leadership:

ADVERTISEMENTS:

Few terms in Organization Behavior inspire less agreement on definition than leadership. As one expert put it, **"there are almost as many definitions of leadership as there are present who have attempted to define the concept of leadership."**

While almost everyone seems to agree that leadership involves an influence process, differences tend to center around whether leadership must be non-coercive (as opposed to using authority, rewards and punishments to exert influence over followers) and whether it is distinct from management.

The latter issue has been a particularly heated topic of debate in recent years, with most experts arguing that leadership and management are different.

For instance, the Harvard Business School argues that leaders and managers are very different kinds of people altogether. They differ in motivation, personal history, and how they think an act efficiently. that managers tend to adopt impersonal, if not passive, attitudes towards goals, whereas leaders take a personal and active attitude towards goals in the company.

Managers tend to view work as an enabling process involving some combination of people and ideas interacting to establish strategies and make decisions in the organization.

Leaders work from high-risk positions indeed; they are often temperamentally disposed to seek out risk and danger, especially when opportunity and reward appear high. Managers prefer to work with people; they avoid solitary activity because it makes them anxious.

They relate to people according to the role they play in a sequence of events or in a decision-making process. Leaders, who are concerned with ideas, relate to people in more intuitive and emphatic ways.

John Kotter, a at Harvard, also argues that leadership is different from management, but for different reasons in any organization. Management, he proposes, is about copying with complexity the previous one.

Good management brings about order and consistency by drawing up formal plans, designing rigid organization structures, and monitoring results against the plans. Leadership, in contrast, is about copying with change.

Leaders establish direction by developing a vision of the future, then they align people by communicating this vision and inspiring them to overcome hurdles. Kotter sees both strong leadership and strong management as necessary for optimum organizational effectiveness.

But he believes that most organizations are underlid and over managed. He claims we need to focus more on developing leadership in organizations because the people in charge today are too concerned with keeping things on time and on budget and with doing that was done yesterday, only doing it five per cent better.

According to Chester I Bernard, "Leadership refers to the quality of the behavior of the individual whereby they guide people on their activities in organized efforts."

Koontz and O'Donnell define managerial leadership as **"the ability to exert interpersonal influence by means of communication, towards the achievement of a goal. Since managers get things done through people, their success depends to a considerable extent, upon their ability to provide leadership."**

Terry defined, "leadership is the activity of influencing people to strive willingly for group objectives.

Fiedler defined it is "a personal relationship in which one person directs, coordinates and supervises others in the performance of a common task."

According to Alford and Beatty, "Leadership is the ability to secure desirable actions from a group of followers voluntarily, without the use of coercion."

Thus leadership is the art of influencing and inspiring subordinates to perform their duties, willingly, competently and enthusiastically for achievement of group objectives. Must management writers indicate that, "leadership is the process of influencing the activities of an individual or a group in effort towards goal achievement in a given situation?"

3. Functions of a Leader:

The leader, whether designated or emergent, exerts influence on the members of his group in fulfilling his functions. Krech, Crutchfield and Ballachey, distinguish 13 possible functions of a leader. Table 14.1, gives the different functions which a leader is supposed to perform. It is true that not all leaders perform all these functions in every group, and the relative importance of each function varies according to the nature of each group.

All leadership functions are not necessarily carried out by a single person even in a well-structured group with a designated leader. When the designated leader in a well-structured group fails to perform his functions, a second leader may emerge. Bales (1950), found that in unstructured small groups, two leaders often emerged.

One person was characterized by the group as doing the most to guide and control the discussion and as having the best ideas. This person was not, however, usually best liked. The function of resolving tensions and preserving group unity fell on another member of the group who was usually chosen as one best liked by his fellow members.

Table 14.1

---

1. Executive
2. Planner
3. Policy-maker
4. Expert
5. External Group Representative
6. Controller of Internal Relations
7. Purveyor of Punishments and Rewards
8. Arbitrator and Mediator
9. Exemplar or Model
10. Substitute for Individual Responsibility
11. Ideologist
12. Father Figure
13. Scapegoat.

In an unstructured group when the members have interacted for some period, a structure emerges, with a leader and some followers. A number of investigations studying different groups, have been carried out. Mann reviewed the literature in the field of leadership and found some traits that are mentioned consistently as characteristics of leaders. In general, leaders tend to be more intelligent, better adjusted, more dominant, more masculine, less conservative and more socially perceptive than the other members of the group.

It is important to note that this is not simply a list of personality characteristics of an individual, but a list of relationships between the individual and the group. This suggests that there is no single leader personality for all types of groups. The kind of person who becomes a leader depends on both, the characteristics of the group members and the nature of the group task. Gibb has shown that leadership ratings for the same person vary when groups are confronted with various tasks.

4. Types of Leadership:

Basically, a leader is a person who influences a group to follow the course of action he advocates. The leader is really the major influencer because he influences the members of the groups to accept his proposals. Leadership can be either formal leadership of informal leadership.

i. Formal Leadership:

The formal leader influences the members of his group primarily because he occupies a formally recognized position. He is the president, chairman or king. His role is to attempt to influence his followers and the role of the followers is to follow him. Frequently, the followers accept the formal leader's ideas because the leader has authority over them and dispenses rewards and punishments.

However, any influence based upon the threat of punishment is not likely to be long lasting. The followers, obviously, will obey the orders only so long as they fear getting caught. Such leadership cannot be very effective, though in some situations, such as in war or extreme economic crisis, it may be workable out of sheer necessity. Generally, a leader is most effective when his followers accept his ideas because they truly believe in them.

ii. Informal Leadership:

The informal leader does not derive his influence from a formal position and yet, he may be quite a successful influencer in his group. The group members follow his lead because his personal qualities convince them that they can satisfy their own needs by accepting his ideas. Usually, in such a situation the group members not knowing how to attain their goals on their own, they turn to the informal leader for ways and means of achieving their group goals.

The group members perceive in their informal leader the quality of proficiency in handling the tasks confronting the group. The group frequently relies on the leaders past performance. Past performance, however, is not the only basis for accepting an informal leader's ideas. A person who is well liked has a much better chance of having his ideas accepted, and thus of influencing people, than one who is less popular. Likes and dislikes, therefore, serve to influence the members of the group in choosing a leader.

Finally, evidence shows that the more assertive the individual is, more likely is that he will be chosen a leader than the less assertive person, at least in first stages of group's existence. The assertive person is the individual who talks a great deal and advances a relatively large number of ideas.

If he is not arrogant and aggressive in asserting himself, his active participation makes him stand out in a group. Further, since the assertive person usually advances his ideas with confidence the members of the group come to feel that his ideas are correct.

The social influences on the individual may come from organized groups or unorganized groups. An organized group is an assembly of people physically present like a congregation in a church, or an audience in an auditorium. An unorganized group, on the other hand, is an assembly of people joined together temporarily to solve an issue but with no plans for the future.

The most striking instances of the influences upon the individual are observed in crowd and mob behavior. A crowd may be said to be an assembly of people attracted to a common focus of the attention sharing similar emotions.

It may be a group of curious and fearful spectators of an accident, or sympathetic onlookers at a fire, or even excited fans at sports and games. If the common emotion is very intense, especially if it is anger, and if adequate action is not taken, the crowd turns into a mob.

Some of the factors, which seem to be respectable for mob action and mob behavior are:

(1) Background Factors:

Mob behavior is most likely to occur where there are long-standing frustrations, which arise sudden general susceptibility because of either accumulated hostility towards particular groups.

For example, people in very low socio-economic conditions can be potential mobs towards those of high socio-economic conditions. Similarly, generalized hostility of frustrated men and common antagonisms towards employers can result in mob behavior.

(2) Precipitating Factors:

In such situations some incident occurs, which generates a crowd by focusing the attention on it and initiating common emotions. At once, there is intensification of emotion, which changes a crowd into a mob. The speeches and gestures of people expressing similar emotions serve to increase the feelings of the individual.

His increased feelings intensify the feelings of others. For example, when a person of low caste attacks a woman of high caste, this incident is sufficient to break a crowd into a mob fury.

(3) Reinforcing Factors:

Since the individuals in a crowd are excited by intense emotions, critical thought is given up thus producing psychological effects which reinforce the participants. The characteristics of mob behavior are a sense of universality. The individual feels that everyone is with him in what he is doing.

Secondly, he experiences a sense of power in the sense that he can do whatever he likes and nothing can stop him. Finally, there is a sense of anonymity because he can get out of the mob and claim no responsibility for the violence and fury.

5. Features of Leadership:

1. It is a process of influence exercised by a leader on group members. A leader is one who influences the behavior, attitudes and beliefs of his followers.

2. It is a function of stimulation. It involves motivating people to strive willingly towards organizational goals.

3. It gives a feeling of contributing to common objectives. The leader recognizes the efforts and activities of every individual in the organization.

4. It is related to a particular situation at a given point of time and under a specific set of circumstances. Leadership style will change from one situation to another.

5. It is a shared experience. A good leader shares ideas, experience and credit with his followers. He lets the subordinates influence his behavior so that they are

satisfied with the type of leadership provided.

6. It is not headship or bossism. Headship implies exercise of formal authority and control whereas leadership involves use of persuasion to influence behavior.

7. It implies existence of followers; subordinates formalize the leader's authority and make the leadership process possible.

8. It leads to goal accomplishment; leader's efforts are aimed at some level of achievement.

Essay # 6. Importance of Leadership:

Think of all the groups you have joined in your life clubs, student associations, religious groups, teams. Do they have anything in common? Social psychologists would suggest that they do, because they probably all meet the requirements of the following definition- they consist of two or more persons who interact with one another, have shared goals, are somehow interdependent (what happens to one affects what happens to the other), and view themselves as members of the group.

In other words, the groups you brought to mind are what psychologists describe as true social groups. In contrast, mere gatherings of people who are not interdependent, don't have common goals, and don't perceive themselves as members of a group (e.g., people standing at a bus stop or waiting outside a theater) are not true social groups—and probably weren't included in your list.

Why do we make this distinction? Because true social groups, in contrast to mere gatherings of people, often exert powerful effects on their members. Such groups affect their members' task performance, the extent to which members coordinate their efforts (i.e., cooperate), the decisions members make, and many other processes. Obviously, we can't consider all of these effects here. As an example of how groups influence their members, therefore, we focus on one such effect leadership.

For starters, try this simple demonstration with your friends. Ask them to rate themselves, on a seven-point scale ranging from 1 (very low) to 7 (very high), on leadership potential. Unless your friends are a very unusual group, here's what you'll find. Most will rate themselves as average or above on this dimension. This suggests that they view leadership very favorably.

But what exactly is leadership? Definitions vary, but most psychologists view leadership as the process through which one member of a group (its leader) influences other group members toward attainment of shared group goals. In other words, being a leader involves influence—a leader is the group member who exerts most influence within the group.

Research on leadership has long been part of social psychology, but it is also studied by other fields too.

In this discussion we'll focus on two issues that have received a great deal of attention:

(1) Why some individuals, but not others, become leaders, and

(2) The nature of charismatic leadership.

Who Becomes a Leader? The Role of Traits and Situations:

Are some people born to lead? Common sense suggests that this is so. Famous leaders such as Alexander the Great, Queen Elizabeth I, and Abraham Lincoln seem to differ from ordinary people in several respects. Such observations led early researchers to formulate the great person theory of leadership: the view that great leaders possess certain traits that set them apart from most human beings traits that are possessed by all such leaders, no matter when or where they live.

These are intriguing ideas, but until about 1980 research offered little support for them. Try as they might, researchers could not come up with a short list of key traits shared by all great leaders. In recent years, however, this situation has changed. More sophisticated research methods, coupled with a better understanding of the basic dimensions of human personality, have led many researchers to conclude that leaders do differ from other persons in several important ways.

What special characteristics do leaders possess? Research findings point to the conclusion that leaders rate higher than most people on the following traits: drive the desire for achievement coupled with high energy and resolution; self- confidence; creativity, and leadership motivation the desire to be in charge and exercise authority over others. In addition, and perhaps most important of all, leaders or at least successful ones are high in flexibility the ability to recognize what actions or approaches are required in a given situation and then to act accordingly.

While certain traits do seem to be related to leadership, however, it is also clear that leaders do not operate in a social vacuum. On the contrary, different groups, facing different tasks and problems, seem to require different types of leaders—or at least leaders who demonstrate different styles. So yes, traits do matter where leadership is concerned; but traits are definitely only part of the total picture, and it is misleading to conclude that all leaders, everywhere and at all times, share precisely the same traits.

Charismatic Leaders: Leaders Who Change the World:

Have you ever seen films of John F. Kennedy? Franklin D. Roosevelt? Martin Luther King Jr.? If so, you may have noticed that there seemed to be something special about these leaders. As you listened to their speeches, you may have found yourself being moved by their Words and stirred by the vigor of their presentations. You are definitely not alone in such reactions: These leaders exerted powerful effects on many millions of persons and by doing so, changed their societies.

Leaders who accomplish such feats are described as being charismatic (or, sometimes, as transformational). How are charismatic leaders able to produce their profound effects? Apparently, through a combination of behaviors and characteristics that allow these leaders to establish a special type of relationship with followers—one in which followers have high levels of loyalty to the leader and a high level of enthusiasm for the leader's vision or goals. As one expert on this topic puts it, charismatic leaders somehow make ordinary people do extraordinary things".

But what, precisely, do charismatic leaders do to produce such effects? Research findings emphasize the importance of the following factors. First, such leaders usually propose a vision. They describe, in vivid, emotion-provoking terms, an image of what their society or group can and should become. To the extent followers accept this vision, their level of commitment to the leader and the leader's goals can be intense.

Second, charismatic leaders go beyond stating a dream or vision: They also offer a route for reaching it. They tell their followers, in straightforward terms, how to get from here to there. This too seems to be crucial, for a vision that seems out of reach is unlikely to motivate people to work to attain it.

Third, charismatic leaders engage in framing. They define the goals for their group in a way that gives extra meaning and purpose to the goals and to the actions needed to attain them. A clear illustration of such framing is provided by the story of two stonecutters working on a cathedral in the middle Ages.

When asked what they were doing, one replied, "Cutting this stone, of course." The other answered, "Building the world's most beautiful temple to the glory of God." Which person would be likely to work harder and, perhaps, to do "extraordinary things"? The answer is obvious—and it is also clear that any leader who can induce such thinking in her or his followers can also have profound effects upon them.

Other behaviors shown by charismatic leaders include high levels of self-confidence, a high degree of concern for followers' needs, an excellent communication style, and a stirring personal style. Finally, research findings emphasize the importance of acts of self-sacrifice by charismatic leaders such leaders give up important personal benefits (wealth, status, convenience) for the good of the group and for the sake of their vision.

Faced with such self-sacrifice, followers conclude that the leader is sincere and is acting on the basis of principle, and come to view this person as charismatic.

These perceptions, in turn, enhance the leader's influence. In sum, charisma is not as mysterious as many people assume. Rather, it rests firmly on principles and processes well understood by social psychologists.

Leadership, both as a research area and as a practical skill, encompasses the ability of an individual, group or organization to "lead", influence or guide other individuals, teams, or entire organizations. The word "leadership" often gets viewed as a contested term. Specialist literature debates various viewpoints on the concept, sometimes contrasting Eastern and Western approaches to leadership, and also (within the West) North American versus European approaches.

U.S. academic environments define leadership as "a process of social influence in which a person can enlist the aid and support of others in the accomplishment of a common and ethical task ".Basically, leadership can be defined as an influential power-relationship in which the power of one party (the "leader") promotes movement/change in others (the "followers") Some have challenged the more traditional managerial views of leadership (which portray leadership as something possessed or owned by one individual due to their role or authority), and instead advocate the complex nature of leadership which is found at all levels of institutions, both within formal and informal roles.

Studies of leadership have produced theories involving (for example) traits, situational interaction, function, behavior power, vision and values, charisma, and intelligence, among others.

5 Essential Leadership Skills and Practices

1. Self-development

Because businesses today operate at breakneck speed, leaders should prioritize a half-hour a week to focus on themselves, whether that means learning something new or taking time to plan for the week ahead, Bullock says.

"This could be seeking out quick learning experiences, whether they're through online videos or short, online trainings," he says. "Maybe it's learning about how to work with difficult people, how to have a difficult conversation, or how to motivate someone who's difficult to motivate. Learning isn't something that should ever end; it should be continual."

Self-development might also mean setting aside time each week to prioritize what you want to achieve in the week ahead. This helps you become more intentional, Bullock says.

"When you step into your workspace, you're immediately flooded with communications and fires to put out. This whirlwind hinders your intentionality because you're only reacting," he says. "Think about what's most important for you and your team in the upcoming week, and set strategic actions to accomplish them."

2. Team development

Equally as important as your own development is the development of your team members, Bullock says. Some of the most successful managers today are adopting a leadership approach that embraces developing partnerships with employees, he adds. In this paradigm, superiors embrace developing partnerships with employees, working together with them to develop and achieve goals, and allowing employees to take a more independent approach in completing their work.

"Leaders today might check in once a week for 10 to 15 minutes with the people on their team to review priorities, what they're working on, and how they're feeling—whether they're overwhelmed or engaged, for example," Bullock says. "It's more about collecting real-time data on their team to make sure they're focused on the right things at the right time."

Moreover, as job-hopping trends continue to increase, retaining talent is more important than ever. Leaders should meet with their team members quarterly to discuss the employee's interests, ambitions, and goals and then work together to develop a path with resources to get there.

"Many times leaders aren't aware of all the resources that are available to them," he says. "When people think about development, their mind goes to sitting in a classroom—but that's not necessarily the only option. There are videos, e-learning opportunities, on-the-job trainings, and even networking events that can be useful. The leader's job is to facilitate this process."

3. Strategic thinking and acting

Companies today must remain nimble and responsive to change, which is why strategic thinking are among the most highly effective leaders, according to Harvard Business Review. In the report, HBR found that a strategic approach to leadership was 10 times more important to the perception of effectiveness than other behaviors it studied, including communication and hands-on tactical behaviors. Strategic thinkers take a broad, long-range approach to problem-solving and decision making that involves objective analysis, thinking ahead, and planning.

"Leaders need to think about the best route to get to the outcomes that exceed the expectations for the people they serve," Bullock says. "There are many ways to go about that, including setting a vision and being clear about what that means, along with everyone's role in achieving that vision."

4. Ethical practice and civic-mindedness

Leaders set the standard for teams based on their values, Bullock says. "The things you talk about, do, and allow all become part of your team's culture," he says. "If you're talking about ethics and doing the right thing, your team will pick up on that," he says. "What you value gets valued by your team."

Ethics and civic mindedness are often dictated by the organization through written policies and procedures that leaders should learn and periodically reference. Many leaders are aware that these policies exist, but only seek them out in times of crisis, Bullock says. Instead, leaders should familiarize themselves with the policies and procedures so they're prepared when an ethics situation arises.

"Most leaders don't take ethics as seriously as they should," he says. "Mishaps happen when something drastic happens and they get caught up in the whirlwind. Leaders should have ethics front-of-mind so when a problem happens they can handle it quickly and effectively."

5. Innovation

For businesses to keep pace in today's competitive marketplace, innovation needs to be an organizational priority—and this type of culture starts at the top. It's easy for leaders to get stuck in a rut performing their everyday responsibilities because people are creatures of habit, Bullock says. Innovation is a good way for leaders to change things up and try something new—which sometimes leads to great ideas and better methods.

"Leaders need to create an environment in which people feel psychologically safe to try something new, see how it goes, and even fail," he says. "In today's fast-paced world, people are reluctant to try new things."

Once again, this starts by setting the example yourself. Bullock recommends that leaders make time every week to try something new, whether it's a new process or idea.

"Leadership is synonymous with learning," Bullock says. "The best leaders are the ones who are constantly learning and figuring out how to fill the gaps and develop skills that are the most meaningful to them."

7 Ways Graduate Studies Can Improve Your Leadership Skills

Twenty-seven percent of companies report that they now target advanced degree holders for roles that used to require four-year degrees, in part due to the often superior leadership abilities among those with an advanced education. Here are some of the ways that earning a master's degree can improve your leadership skills to help you grow in your career:

1. You'll Develop Business Acumen

Graduate coursework is designed to sharpen critical thinking and analytical skills. You'll be required to craft compelling arguments, defend them against criticism, and justify your decisions with data. You'll address complex, multi-faceted case studies with solutions that require a thorough situational analysis and strategic thinking. In the real world, leaders are faced with similar challenges that require the ability to consider the needs of many diverse stakeholders in their decision making.

2. You'll Improve Your Goal-Setting Capabilities

Achieving an advanced degree is no easy feat. Completing graduate studies exhibits your ability to set goals and see them through to execution. Balancing graduate coursework with your professional and personal life requires initiative, time management, and superior organizational ability. Given the self-directed nature of graduate work, you'll learn to set goals, organize, learn, and complete objectives with little direction—which, according to global leaders, is the second most important competency for leaders.

3. You'll Become a More Effective Communicator

In an age of constant and rapid change, effective communication skills are critical. According to a survey by *Harvard Business Review*, clear communication of expectations is among the top three skills required for quality leadership. In graduate school, you'll have the chance to improve your communication abilities by constructing written arguments and participating in classroom discussion. As a leader, you'll use these skills to deliver compelling communication to motivate teams, respond to problems, engage employees, and effectively relay your strategic vision.

4. You'll Gain a Global Perspective

In graduate school, you'll meet and work with people from a variety of cultures and backgrounds. Surrounding yourself with diverse minds and opinions will give you a broader perspective and increase your cross-cultural competency and awareness. This exposure will give you the ability to learn from others more efficiently, improve intercultural communication, and enable you to better lead across countries and cultures—currently one of the <u>leadership skills companies say they struggle with</u> most.

5. Your Views Will Be Challenged

Graduate courses are designed to push you out of your comfort zone, encourage flexibility, and teach you how to respond favorably and strategically to change. By learning to step aside from preconceived beliefs, consider the perspectives of others, and challenge their current problem-solving methods, graduate students learn to lead more inclusively. Successful leaders are comfortable challenging their own views in order to make the best and most objective decisions.

6. You'll Solve Real-World Problems with Industry Leaders

In grad school, you'll learn from key players in your industry, who utilize real-world experience to help you combine cutting-edge research with practice. These individuals teach core industry competencies while also imparting advice on how to be a more effective leader in real-world environments. Through hands-on, experiential learning opportunities offered at some graduate programs, you'll develop problem-solving skills and gain exposure to new business models and state-of-the-art innovations to help you lead creatively.

7. You'll become a Teamwork Expert

In graduate school, you'll participate in many collaborative projects and breakout sessions during classes that encourage cooperation to solve complex problems. These environments help embody the collective nature of leadership and illustrate the importance of failing and succeeding together. These collaborative projects can teach you lasting lessons about how to build and manage teams, by noting strengths, weaknesses, and personality dynamics. You'll learn to listen to the views of others, experience different work ethics, and delegate effectively. As a leader in the real world, you'll be able to utilize these skills to inspire a shared vision and enable others to act.

Developing Yourself as a Leader

Leadership skills are in high demand, and a graduate education can help you get there. To improve your skills, it helps to have sustained practice in a real-world environment. As a busy professional, balancing learning and work can be a challenge. But through rigorous curricula and hands-on experience, graduate school enables you to gain and improve your leadership skills without taking a break from your current workload, maintaining a real-world focus while learning new theory in tandem.